# Microw

# Masterchef!

40 Mouth-Watering Microwave Recipes

to Celebrate National Microwave

Oven Day

BY

*Daniel Humphreys*

# License Notes

No part of this Book can be reproduced in any form or by any means including print, electronic, scanning or photocopying unless prior permission is granted by the author.

All ideas, suggestions and guidelines mentioned here are written for informative purposes. While the author has taken every possible step to ensure accuracy, all readers are advised to follow information at their own risk. The author cannot be held responsible for personal and/or commercial damages in case of misinterpreting and misunderstanding any part of this Book

# Table of Contents

# Introduction

On December 6th, the nation celebrates National Microwave Oven Day. It's the perfect opportunity to give one of the most used appliances in your kitchen a time to shine.

Ever since the microwave oven first appeared on sale to the public in the mid-1970s, it changed the way millions of people prepare their food.

So let's take a look at how the appliance that revolutionized our kitchens found pride of place on our kitchen countertop.

In 1945, American engineer Percy Spencer invented the microwave by sheer accident. While working in a lab testing magnetrons Percy noticed that a candy bar in his trouser pocket had started to melt, thanks to the high-powered vacuum tubes inside radars. Very soon afterward, the microwave pinged into life.

One year later and the very first commercial microwave was tested in a Boston restaurant in 1946.

When microwave ovens first went on sale, they cost a staggering $5000, making them way out of the budget of most modern homes.

Seven years later, the price had come down to between $2000-3000 compared to the cost of a new car at $1700.

However, by the mid-sixties, the first relatively low energy microwave model went on the market at $500.

The rest, as they say, is history and today, a staggering 90 percent of home cooks in the United States own a microwave oven!

There has never been a better time to become a microwave masterchef. Far from merely heating, re-heating or thawing food, a microwave is perfect for preparing mouth-watering meals from scratch.

This year on National Microwave Oven Day discover 40 mouth-watering microwave recipes.

# Appetizers and Lite Bites

# Beef and Cheese Enchiladas

This easy Mexican dish takes the minimum of hassle to prepare and is super satisfying.

**Servings:** 2-3

**Total Time:** 30mins

**Ingredients:**

- ½ pound ground beef
- 2 tbsp onion (peeled, chopped)
- 2 cups Cheddar cheese (shredded, divided)
- 1 (10 ounce) can enchilada sauce (divided)
- 1 tbsp canned chopped green chilies
- 6 (6") corn tortillas (warm)
- Lettuce (shredded, to serve)
- Sour cream (to serve)

**Directions:**

1. Crumble the ground beef into a microwave-safe dish or 2-quart capacity.

2. Add the onion, and covered, microwave on high for 2-3 minutes, until the beef is no longer pink. Drain.

3. Stir in the shredded cheese followed by ¼ cup of enchilada sauce and the green chilies.

4. Add ½ cup of the beef mixture off center on each of the warm tortillas.

5. Roll the tortillas up and arrange them in a greased 11x7" microwave-safe dish, seam side facing downwards. Top with the remaining enchilada sauce.

6. Microwave, covered and on high for 5-6 minutes until heated through.

7. Garnish with the remaining cheese, cover, and microwave for 1-2 minutes, until the cheese melts.

8. Serve with torn lettuce and a dollop of sour cream.

# Chicken Teriyaki

Forget ordering that take-out, instead, stay indoors and prepare this tasty chicken dish for two.

**Servings:** 2

**Total Time:** 10mins

**Ingredients:**

- 2 tbsp ketchup
- ¼ cup soy sauce
- White sugar (to taste)
- 2 tbsp garlic powder
- 1 (8 ounce) skinless, boneless chicken breast half (cut into strips)

**Directions:**

1. Add the ketchup, soy sauce, sugar (to taste), and garlic powder to a bowl.

2. Add the chicken and toss to coat evenly.

3. Place the chicken on a microwave-safe plate.

4. Cove the plate with kitchen wrap and on high, cook for between 5-8 minutes, until the chicken is opaque in the middle and its juices run clear.

# Crab Stuffed Mushrooms

In less than 10 minutes, these mushrooms stuffed with sweet crab meat and cream cheese are a perfect party snack or appetizer to share.

**Servings:** 4-6

**Total Time:** 8mins

**Ingredients:**

- 1 pound mushroom caps
- 8-10 ounces cream cheese (softened)
- 1(14 ounce) package imitation crab meat (shredded)
- Lemon pepper (to season)
- Butter

**Directions:**

1. First, clean the mushrooms by wiping them with a dampened kitchen paper towel. Break off the stems and discard.

2. In a bowl, combine the cream cheese with the crabmeat. Adjust the amount of cream cheese according to your preference.

3. Season to taste, with lemon pepper.

4. Add 5-6 dabs of butter to the bottom of a microwave-safe glass baking dish.

5. Stuff the mixture into each mushroom cap and place the stuffed mushrooms on top of the butter.

6. Cover with kitchen wrap and microwave on high, for 4-5 minutes, until the mushrooms are cooked through.

7. Enjoy.

# Eggplant Parmigiana

A flavorsome eggplant parmigiana served with garlic bread and a glass of Italian red wine makes a tasty and satisfying lunch.

**Servings:** 4-6

**Total Time:** 25mins

**Ingredients:**

- 1 (1¼ pound) eggplant
- 1 large egg
- 1 tbsp olive oil
- ⅓ cup Italian breadcrumbs
- 1 tbsp cornmeal
- 6 tbsp Parmesan cheese (grated)
- 2 cups thick, store-bought, marinara spaghetti sauce
- 1 ½ cups mozzarella cheese

**Directions:**

1. Slice the eggplant crosswise into slices approximately ½" thick.

2. In a bowl, beat the egg with the oil.

3. In a shallow bowl, blend the breadcrumbs with the cornmeal and 3 tbsp of grated Parmesan cheese.

4. Dip each slice of eggplant first in the egg, before dredging in the breadcrumbs to evenly coat.

5. Arrange the slices, in a 12" circular baking dish. They need to overlap.

6. Cover the dish with kitchen paper towel and on high, cook for between 10-14 minutes, until the eggplant is fork tender.

7. Remove from the microwave and spoon the sauce over the eggplant.

8. Scatter the mozzarella over the top followed by the remaining grated Parmesan.

9. Uncovered, and on high, microwave for 5 minutes, until the cheeses are entirely melted.

# Minestrone Soup

Enjoy a big bowl of veggie-packed minestrone. Enjoy all the taste of this Italian soup with none of the fuss.

**Servings:** 4

**Total Time:** 18mins

**Ingredients:**

- 1 cup carrots (sliced)
- 1 cup celery (sliced)
- 1 cup zucchini (sliced)
- ½ cup sweet yellow pepper (diced)
- 1 small onion (peeled, chopped)
- 1 tbsp olive oil
- 1 (15 ounce) can cannellini beans (rinsed, drained)
- 1 (14½ ounce) can beef broth
- 1 (14½ ounce) can diced tomatoes
- 1 cup medium pasta shells (cooked, drained)
- ½-1 tsp dried basil
- ½ tsp salt
- ¼ tsp pepper

**Directions:**

1. In a microwave-safe bowl of a 2-quart capacity, combine the carrots with the celery, zucchini, pepper, and onion. Drizzle with olive oil and toss to coat evenly.

2. Cover with a lid and on high, microwave for 3 minutes.

3. Stir in the cannellini beans, beef broth, tomatoes, pasta, basil, and seasoning.

4. Cover and on high, cook for 8-10 minutes.

5. Serve with crusty bread.

# Paneer Tikka

Crispy pieces of cottage cheese infused with spices is the perfect dinner-party appetizer to serve as part of an Indian feast.

**Servings:** 6

**Total Time:** 2hours 20mins

**Ingredients:**

- 1½ cups thick curds
- 3 tsp chili powder
- 1½ tsp ginger or garlic paste
- 1½ tsp fenugreek
- 1½ tsp amchur powder
- 3 tsp oil
- 10½ ounces paneer (cut into 1 ½ "cubes)
- Salt

**Directions:**

1. Add the curds, chili powder, ginger paste, fenugreek, amchur powder and oil to a bowl. Stir to combine.

2. Add the cubes of paneer and set aside to marinate for 2 hours.

3. Remove from the marinade, transfer to a microwave-safe plate and microwave on full power for 3 minutes.

4. Season, serve and enjoy.

# Risotto Primavera

Who needs a ready-meal when you can create a creamy risotto in no time at all?

**Servings:** 4

**Total Time:** 25mins

**Ingredients:**

- 12¼ ounces risotto rice
- ¾ cup white wine
- 3½ cups hot vegetable stock (divided)
- 1 pound 2 ounces frozen pea and bean mixed vegetables
- 1 (3½ ounce) pack of asparagus
- 3½ ounces soft goats' cheese
- Mint leaves (torn)

**Directions:**

1. Add the rice to a microwave-safe bowl.

2. Pour the wine over the rice along with 1/3 of the hot vegetable stock.

3. Cover the bowl with kitchen wrap and on high, microwave for 10 minutes.

4. Stir, and pour in an additional 1/3 of the stock.

5. Recover and microwave for another 3 minutes.

6. Stir, and add the frozen veggies, asparagus, and the remaining stock.

7. Recover and microwave for an additional 7 minutes.

8. Stir in the cheese along with a handful of torn mint.

9. Allow the risotto to stand for a couple of minutes, before serving.

# Sea Scallops and Mushrooms

Nothing could be easier than seasoned sea scallops prepared in the microwave.

**Servings:** 2-4

**Total Time:** 12mins

**Ingredients:**

- 1 pound frozen sea scallops (thawed, rinsed, patted dry)
- 12 small fresh mushrooms (halved)
- 1 tbsp white wine
- 1½ tsp freshly squeezed lemon juice
- ½ tsp lemon pepper seasoning
- ¼ tsp dried thyme
- ⅛ tsp garlic powder
- ⅛ tsp seasoned salt
- 2 tsp butter (melted)

**Directions:**

1. Add the scallops and mushrooms to a 9" microwave-safe glass dish.

2. In a bowl, combine the white wine with the fresh lemon juice, lemon pepper seasoning, thyme, garlic powder, and seasoned salt. Pour the mixture over the scallops.

3. Cover the bowl, and on 50 percent power, microwave for 2 minutes.

4. Remove from the microwave, and stir.

5. Recover and microwave on 50 percent power for an additional 4 - 4 ½ minutes, until the scallops are opaque.

6. Stir in the melted butter and serve.

# Salmon Mousse

A sophisticated and elegant appetizer to serve with mini toasts or buttered toast.

**Servings:** 4

**Total Time:** 40mins

**Ingredients:**

- Butter (to grease)

**Sauce:**

- 1 tbsp pickled onion (sliced)
- 1 tbsp freshly squeezed lemon juice
- 1 tbsp dry Vermouth
- 1 tbsp olive oil

**Mousse:**

- 3 tbsp water
- ¼ cup milk
- 1 (¼ ounce) envelope unflavored gelatin
- ¼ pound smoked salmon, sliced thinly into 2-inch lengths
- 1 cup of whipping cream
- 1 tsp chervil (to garnish)

**Directions:**

1. Lightly grease 4 molds.

2. In a bowl, combine the pickled onion with the lemon juice, dry Vermouth, and olive oil.

3. To a microwave-safe bowl, add 3 tbsp of water along with the gelatin. Stir and set aside for 5 minutes. On high, microwave for 10-12 seconds to dissolve the gelatin. Timings will vary depending on the wattage of your microwave.

4. Add the smoked salmon, milk and half of the whipping cream to a food processor and process for 10-20 seconds, until smooth.

5. Add the remaining cream and blend. Next, add the dissolved gelatin and process for 10 seconds, until smooth.

6. Evenly divide the mixture between the 4 molds and transfer to the fridge to the chill and set.

7. When you are ready to serve the mousse. Dampen your finger and press the surface of the mousse to allow air to enter between the mousse and the mold.

8. Put a plate on the top of the mold and carefully invert.

9. Serve the mousse with a drizzle of sauce and garnish with some chervil.

# Speedy Baked Brie

No need to waste valuable time baking when you can whip this up in the microwave in just three minutes, making it ideal for those unexpected visitors.

**Servings:** 2-4

**Total Time:** 3mins

**Ingredients:**

- 8 ounces whole Brie
- ¼ cup pecans (roughly chopped)
- ¼ cup pomegranate seeds
- ¼ cup pure maple syrup

**Directions:**

1. Place the unwrapped Brie on a microwave-safe rimmed plate.

2. On high, microwave for approximately 75 seconds, or until the cheese is soft in the center. Take care not to allow the Brie to puff up or burst.

3. Scatter with chopped pecans and pomegranate seeds.

4. Pour the maple syrup over the top.

5. Serve with crackers or crusty bread.

# Mains

# Cashew Chicken

Craving for a Chinese meal, and no oven? It's no problem, this classic take-out dish is easy to prepare and delicious served with either noodles or rice.

**Servings:** 2

**Total Time:** 20mins

## Ingredients:

- 2 boneless chicken breasts (skinned, thinly sliced)
- 2 tbsp soy sauce
- 2 cloves garlic (peeled, minced)
- 1 tbsp cornstarch
- 1 tbsp sherry
- ¼ tsp ginger
- 2½ tbsp oil (heated)
- 1 cup sugar snap peas
- ½ cup cashews

**Directions:**

1. In a microwave-safe bowl, combine the chicken with the soy sauce, garlic, cornstarch, sherry, and ginger.

2. Using a smaller bowl, microwave the oil for between 15-20 seconds until warm.

3. Pour the warm oil over the chicken mixture, stirring to incorporate.

4. On high, microwave for 4-6 minutes, stirring every 60 seconds.

5. Add the peas along with the cashews and cover with kitchen wrap.

6. On high, microwave for 3-4 minutes, until the chicken is cooked through, and the peas are fork tender. Stir after 1½-2 minutes.

7. Allow to stand for 3 minutes before serving with either noodles or rice.

# Cheesy Ham Casserole

A creamy, cheesy ham casserole has everything you need for a satisfying meal.

**Servings:** 2

**Total Time:** 22mins

**Ingredients:**

- 1 (10 ounce) can of cream of mushroom soup
- ⅓ cup whole milk
- 1 cup Cheddar cheese (grated)
- ½ tsp celery salt
- 1 tsp Worcestershire sauce
- 1 (5 ounce) can tender chunk ham (flaked)
- 7 ounces elbow macaroni (cooked, drained)

**Directions:**

1. In the microwave, heat the soup, milk, cheddar cheese, celery salt, and Worcestershire sauce.

2. Add the ham along with the cooked macaroni.

3. Transfer the mixture to a casserole dish and microwave on 70 percent power for 10 minutes.

4. Serve and enjoy.

# Chocolate Chili

A romantic meal for two or date night in, this decadent chocolate chili has lots of heartwarming spices.

**Servings:** 2

**Total Time:** 15mins

**Ingredients:**

- ½ small onion (peeled, finely chopped)
- 1 large clove of garlic (peeled, crushed)
- A knob of butter
- ½ tsp ground cumin
- ½ tsp smoked paprika
- Pinch of chili flakes
- 1 (14½ ounce) can chopped tomatoes (drained, juice reserved)
- 1 (14½ ounce) can kidney beans (drained, rinsed)
- ½ vegetable stock cube
- 2 squares of dark chocolate
- Sour cream (to serve, optional)
- Coriander (to garnish)

**Directions:**

1. Add the onion, garlic, butter, cumin, paprika, and chili flakes to a microwave-safe container, quickly stir, and on high microwave for 30-40 seconds.

2. Allow to stand for 60 seconds, before adding the tomatoes, kidney beans, the vegetable stock cube and squares of chocolate.

3. Cover the container with kitchen wrap and prick the wrap 3 times.

4. Lay a sheet of kitchen paper on the turntable of your microwave.

5. Place the container on top of the paper and on high, cook for 2 minutes.

6. Stir and allow to stand for 60 seconds. You may need to add a drop of the reserved tomato juice if needed.

7. Cover the container, and on a moderate setting, microwave for an additional 2 minutes. Stir and allow to stand for 60 seconds.

8. Add a dollop of sour cream to each serving and garnish with coriander.

# Jambalaya

Ditch the ready-meals and instead make this spicy Cajun-style jambalaya using only a microwave.

**Servings:** 2

**Total Time:** 15mins

**Ingredients:**

- 6½ ounces quick-cook rice
- 1 stock cube
- Salt (to taste)
- ½ tsp chili powder
- ½ ring of chorizo (sliced)
- 1 red pepper (seeded, sliced)
- 2-4 tbsp tomato puree
- Fresh coriander leaves (to serve)

**Directions:**

1. Add the rice, stock cube, and a pinch of salt to a microwave-safe bowl and cover with 14 ounces of water.

2. Place the bowl in the microwave and cook for 2 minutes, stir and continue to cook according to the manufacturer's directions on the packaging, until fluffy. You may need to add a drop more water if necessary.

3. Add the chili powder, slices of chorizo, and red pepper in a microwave-safe bowl and cook for 2 minutes.

4. Add the tomato puree along with the cooked rice.

5. Garnish with coriander and enjoy.

# Mince and Pasta Bake

Your family will love coming homing to this comforting meaty pasta bake.

**Servings:** 6

**Total Time:** 35mins

**Ingredients:**

- 8¾ ounces macaroni
- 1 pound 2 ounces beef mince
- 1 cup onion (peeled, diced)
- 1 cup celery (sliced)
- 1 tbsp garlic (peeled, crushed)
- 1 (14½ ounce) can diced tomatoes
- 1 (10½ ounce) jar pasta sauce
- 1 tbsp sugar
- 1 tbsp paprika
- Pinch of cayenne
- 1 tsp dried oregano
- ¼ tsp caraway seeds
- 1 tsp salt

**Directions:**

1. Cook the macaroni in boiling salted water until al dente. Drain.

2. In the meantime, crumble the minced beef into a microwave-safe casserole dish of 2-quart capacity.

3. Add the onion, along with the celery and garlic and on high, cook in the microwave for between 5-6 minutes, stirring once, until the meat is no longer pink. Drain the fat.

4. Stir in the tomatoes followed by the pasta sauce and sugar. Season with paprika, cayenne pepper, oregano, caraway seeds, and salt.

5. Cover the dish and on level 8, microwave for approximately 12-15 minutes, until the flavors combine.

6. Remove the dish from the microwave and stir in the drained macaroni. Cook for an additional 2-3 minutes, until heated through.

7. Enjoy.

# Peppered Steak

A midweek classic, pepper steak is comforting and delicious.

**Servings:** 2-3

**Total Time:** 30mins

**Ingredients:**

- 2 tbsp olive oil
- 1 pound boneless steak (cut into thin strips)
- ½ tsp salt
- 2 medium red peppers (sliced)
- 2 onions (peeled, sliced)
- 1 tbsp cornstarch
- ½ cup beef broth

**Directions:**

1. Add the olive oil to an 8" microwave-safe dish.

2. On moderate to high heat, microwave for 3 minutes.

3. Add the steak and vegetables to the dish and on moderate-high heat, microwave for 3-4 minutes, until the veggies are tender yet crisp.

4. In a second bowl, blend the cornstarch with the broth until silky smooth.

5. Transfer the mixture to the dish and on moderate to high heat, microwave for 3-4 minutes, until the sauce thickens. Stir once during cooking.

6. Serve.

# Shrimp in Butter Sauce

When time is short, this seafood dish makes a tasty main meal to serve over rice or pasta.

**Servings:** 4

**Total Time:** 10mins

**Ingredients:**

- ½ cup unsalted butter
- ¼ cup freshly squeezed lemon juice
- 2 tbsp white onion (peeled, minced)
- 1 tbsp parsley (chopped)
- ⅓ tsp spice seasoning
- ½ tsp garlic (peeled, minced)
- 1 pound raw shrimp (peeled, deveined)
- 2 cups mushrooms (halved)

**Directions:**

1. In a microwave-safe bowl, combine the butter, lemon juice, white onion, parsley, spice seasoning, and garlic, mix to incorporate and on high, microwave for 90 seconds.

2. Add the shrimp along with the mushrooms.

3. Cover the dish and on high, microwave for 3-4 minutes, or until cooked through.

4. Allow to stand for 2 minutes.

5. Serve and enjoy with rice or pasta.

# Soy Salmon Noodles

Now you don't have to substitute taste for speed. This tasty noodle main has a lot of flavor.

**Servings:** 1

**Total Time:** 18mins

**Ingredients:**

- 1 (4 ½ ounce) salmon fillet
- 2 tbsp orange juice, fresh or from concentrate
- 1 tbsp soy sauce
- 1 tsp honey
- 1 nest of noodles
- 2 tbsp frozen peas
- 1 spring onion, (finely sliced)
- 2 tsp sesame seeds

**Directions:**

1. Add the salmon to a microwave-safe bowl. Pour the orange juice and soy sauce over the salmon. Drizzle the salmon with honey and transfer to the microwave, cooking for 4 minutes, and remembering to flip halfway through the cooking process. Allow to rest in the microwave for 6 seconds, before serving.

2. Place the noodles in a microwave-safe bowl, pour in sufficient boiling water to cover, and microwave until cooked, approximately 5 minutes.

3. Add the frozen peas and set aside for 2-3 minutes, to defrost. Drain.

4. Arrange the salmon on top of the noodles.

5. Pour the sauce over the noodles and garnish with spring onion and sesame seeds.

# Spanish Omelet

Looking for a speedy, inexpensive and healthy meal, then this veggie-packed omelet will tick all your boxes.

**Servings:** 4

**Total Time:** 15mins

**Ingredients:**

- 1 onion (peeled, finely chopped)
- 1 red pepper (seeded, cut into rings)
- 1¾ ounces mushrooms (finely sliced)
- 14ounces potatoes (peeled, sliced)
- 1¾ ounces frozen peas
- 4 large free-range eggs
- 1 tsp grain mustard
- Black pepper
- 1 ounce low-fat mature Cheddar cheese
- Crusty bread (to serve)

**Directions:**

1. Add the onion, pepper, and mushrooms to a microwave-safe dish, cover with kitchen wrap, leaving a small area uncovered, and on full power, cook for 4 minutes.

2. Remove the dish from the microwave, remove the veggies and transfer to a bowl.

3. Add the potatoes to a microwave-safe dish, and cover with kitchen wrap, leaving a small area uncovered, and on full power, cook for 6 minutes. Set aside to stand for 2 minutes, checking that the slices are soft. If not, cook on full power for an additional 60 seconds.

4. Add the peas to a colander. Pour boiling water over the peas, to soften. Drain.

5. Crack the 4 eggs into a bowl, whisking well with the mustard and a dash of black pepper. Whisk until frothy.

6. In the microwave-safe dish, combine the potatoes with the veggie mixture and peas. Pour the eggs over the top.

7. Sprinkle the grated cheese over the top of the eggs and cook on full power for 2 minutes. Remove the dish and stir the outside parts of the mixture into the middle, and using a spoon, flatten. Cook for an additional 2 minutes. Remove the dish and stirring the outside parts of the mixture in the middle and with a spoon as before, flatten.

8. Cook for an additional 2 minutes. Remove from the microwave, cover with kitchen wrap and set aside to stand for 2 minutes. If the egg yolk is a little runny, cook for an additional 60 seconds on full power.

9. Cut the omelet into wedges and serve with crusty bread.

# Steak with Peppers

Yes, you can microwave steak, and what's more, it's delicious too.

**Servings:** 2-3

**Total Time:** 25mins

**Ingredients:**

- 2 tbsp olive oil
- 1 pound boneless steak (cut into thin strips)
- ½ tsp salt
- 2 medium red peppers (sliced)
- 2 onions (peeled, sliced)
- 1 tbsp cornstarch
- ½ cup beef broth

**Directions:**

1. Add the olive oil to an 8" microwave-safe dish.

2. On moderate to high heat, microwave for 3 minutes.

3. Add the steak to the dish and on moderate-high heat, microwave for between 7-8 minutes. Stirring once.

4. Next, add the salt, peppers, and onions and cover with kitchen wrap. On moderate to high, microwave for 3-4 minutes, until the veggies are tender yet crisp.

5. In a second bowl, blend the cornstarch with the broth until silky smooth.

6. Transfer the mixture to the dish and on moderate to high heat, microwave for 3-4 minutes, until the sauce thickens. Stir once during cooking.

7. Serve.

# Sides, Dips, and Sauces

# Acorn Squash with Dates

Everyone will love this veggie side dish. Its sweet flavor is the perfect complement to roast meat and poultry.

**Servings:** 4

**Total Time:** 25mins

**Ingredients:**

- 1 (2 pound) acorn squash
- 2 tbsp dates (chopped)
- 1 tbsp packed brown sugar
- 1½ tsp vegetable oil spread

**Directions:**

1. Pierce the squash in several places with a knife, this will allow the steam to escape.

2. Put the squash on a piece of kitchen paper and uncovered, microwave for 5 minutes, until the squash is warm to the touch.

3. Cut the warm squash in half, remove and discard the seeds.

4. Put the halves of squash in a shallow microwave-safe dish, cut sides facing downwards.

5. Cover with microwave-safe kitchen wrap, folding one corner back to vent the steam.

6. On high, microwave for 5-8 minutes, rotating the dish every 2 minutes, cook until tender.

7. Set aside to rest for 5 minutes.

8. In a bowl, combine dates, brown sugar and spread.

9. Turn the squash with the cut sides facing up.

10. Spoon the date mixture into the middle of the squash, and uncovered, microwave on high for 60 seconds, until the sugar is entirely melted.

11. Slice each half of squash into 2 pieces and serve.

# Asparagus Bruschetta

Forget the tomatoes; asparagus takes center stage for this cheesy baguette side dish.

**Servings:** 4

**Total Time:**

**Ingredients:**

- 24 (2") long asparagus spears
- 1 tbsp water
- Salt
- 1 tsp butter
- 1 tsp parsley (chopped)
- 4 slices of baguette
- 2 tbsp mozzarella cheese (grated)
- Dry red chili flakes

**Directions:**

1. In a microwave-safe bowl, combine the asparagus spears with the 1 tbsp of water and a pinch of salt. On high, microwave for 45 seconds.

2. Remove and put to one side.

3. Combine the butter with the parsley and spread the mixture onto one side of each slice of baguette.

4. Place the buttered slices of baguette on a microwave-safe shallow plate and on high, microwave for 30 seconds.

5. Arrange 6 asparagus spears on each of the 4 slices of bread.

6. Top with grated mozzarella and garnish with red chili flakes. On high, microwave for 30 seconds.

7. Serve.

# Brussels Sprouts with Bacon and Caraway Seeds

Nothing says family or holiday meal like a side dish of Brussels sprouts, and this recipe featuring bacon and caraway seeds will have everyone coming back for more.

**Servings:** 6

**Total Time:** 25mins

**Ingredients:**

- 6 ounces bacon (cut into 4" pieces)
- 3 (10 ounce) packages frozen Brussels sprouts (thawed under running water)
- ¼ cup white wine vinegar
- 1 tbsp caraway seeds
- 1 tsp coarse kosher salt
- Black pepper

**Directions:**

1. Arrange the bacon pieces in a single layer in a microwave-safe 2-quart capacity casserole dish, with a tight-fitting lid.

2. Cover the bowl loosely with kitchen paper and on full power, microwave for 5½ minutes until cooked to your liking. Remove the dish from the microwave.

3. Using a slotted spoon, remove the bacon from the dish and put to one side.

4. Stir in the sprouts, white wine vinegar, and caraway seeds.

5. Cover with the tight-fitting lid and on full power, microwave, while stirring once for 10 minutes.

6. Remove from the microwave and fold in the cooked bacon. Season to taste and serve.

# Creamy Cauliflower Cheese and Bacon

This side dish with sour cream, cheese, and bacon is the best comfort food ever.

**Servings:** 6

**Total Time:** 20mins

**Ingredients:**

- 1 pound cauliflower florets
- ¼ tsp garlic powder
- 3 tbsp butter
- 4 ounces sour cream
- 2 tbsp chives (snipped, divided)
- 1 cup cheddar cheese (grated, divided)
- Salt and pepper
- 2 slices cooked bacon (crumbled)

**Directions:**

1. Add the cauliflower florets to a microwave-safe bowl.

2. Add 2 tbsp of water to the bowl and cover with kitchen wrap. On full power, microwave for between 5-8 minutes, until fork tender. Drain and set aside to rest for 2 minutes.

3. Transfer the cauliflower to a food processor and process until pureed. Next, add the garlic, butter, and sour cream. Process to a mashed potato consistency.

4. Remove the mash from the processor, transfer to a bowl and add the majority of the chives, holding some back to use as a garnish.

5. Add ½ cup of Cheddar cheese and by hand, mix to combine. Season.

6. Top the cauliflower with the remaining ½ cup of cheese, chives, and bacon.

7. Return to the microwave and melt the cheese.

8. Serve.

# Easy Alfredo Sauce

A creamy, cheesy sauce makes an ideal pasta sauce, and this homemade version is far tastier than any jarred version.

**Servings:** 2

**Total Time:** 0mins

**Ingredients:**

- 2 ounces aged Parmesan cheese (cubed)
- 2 ounces aged Romano cheese (cubed)
- 2 ounces aged Asiago cheese (cubed)
- 6 tbsp butter
- 2 cloves garlic (peeled, minced)
- Salt and black pepper
- 1 tsp onion powder
- ½ cup whole milk

**Directions:**

1. Add the Parmesan, Romano and Asiago cheeses, to a food processor. Next, add the butter, and garlic, along with a pinch of salt, a dash of pepper and the onion powder. On the pulse setting, finely grate.

2. Add the cheese mixture along with the butter and milk to a microwave-safe bowl and on high, heat for 60 seconds. Stir to combine.

3. Heat for an additional 60 seconds, and stir.

4. Finally, heat for a final 60 seconds and stir to combine.

5. Pour over your pasta of choice and enjoy.

# Macaroni n' Cheese

Classic combines with convenience. This easy recipe for Mac n' Cheese is ready in less than 30 minutes. Serve as a side order with ribs for a satisfying main meal.

**Servings:** 4

**Total Time:** 17mins

**Ingredients:**

- 1 cup macaroni pasta (uncooked)
- 2 tbsp flour
- ¼ cup onion (peeled, chopped)
- 1 tsp salt
- Dash of Tabasco sauce
- 1 cup milk
- 1 cup water
- 2 tbsp butter
- 1 cup cheese (cubed)

**Directions:**

1. In a casserole dish, combine the pasta with the flour, onion, salt and a dash of Tabasco.

2. Stir in the milk along with the water. Dab with butter and uncovered, cook on high, in the microwave for between 10-12 minutes.

3. Fold in the cheese and allow to stand for 3-5 minutes, to melt the cheese.

# Mexican Beer Cheese Dip

Need a snack for game-night in? No problem, this cheesy Mexican beer side will get everyone chipping n dipping!

**Servings:** 12

**Total Time:** 40mins

**Ingredients:**

- 16 ounces cream cheese (cut into ½ "cubes)
- 6 ounces Mexican beer
- 1 (4½ ounce) can chopped green chilies
- 1 clove garlic (peeled, finely chopped)
- 1 tbsp taco seasoning
- 8 ounces sour cream
- ¼ cup tomato (diced)
- 2 tbsp fresh cilantro leaves (chopped)
- Tortilla chips (to serve)

**Directions:**

1. In a microwave-safe bowl, combine the cheese with the Mexican beer, green chilies, garlic, and taco seasoning mix.

2. Uncovered, microwave on high for 3 minutes, stir to combine, then microwave for an additional 3-5 minutes, until silky smooth.

3. Stir in the sour cream and garnish with diced tomatoes and cilantro.

4. Serve with tortilla chips.

# Pesto-Stuffed Tomatoes

If you are looking for the perfect side dish, then look no further than these stuffed tomatoes.

**Servings:** 4

**Total Time:** 55mins

## Ingredients:

- 1½ pounds large tomatoes
- 2 tbsp Parmesan cheese (freshly shredded)
- 2 tbsp pine nuts
- 2 tbsp fresh basil leaves (chopped)
- 1½ tsp olive oil
- ½ tsp garlic salt
- ¼ tsp pepper
- 2 slices bread (torn into crumbs)
- 1 tbsp Parmesan cheese (shredded)

**Directions:**

1. Cut ¼" slice from the stem of each of the tomatoes, and scoop out the pulp. Discard the tomato seeds and chop the pulp.

2. Combine the pulp with 2 tbsp shredded Parmesan, pine nuts, basil leaves, olive oil, garlic salt, and pepper. Gently stir in the breadcrumbs.

3. Fill the tomato shells with the Parmesan mixture.

4. Arrange the tomatoes in shallow, circular microwave-safe dish. Cover the dish loosely with wax paper.

5. On high, microwave for 3-4 minutes, until fork tender.

6. Garnish with 1 tbsp of shredded Parmesan and allow to stand for a couple of minutes, to melt the cheese.

# Sweet Potato Hummus

Mediterranean hummus gets a microwave makeover. Enjoy as a dip or side and serve with pita or veggie batons.

**Servings:** 8-10

**Total Time:** 2hours 30mins

## Ingredients:

- 1 (12-14 ounce) orange sweet potato
- 1 (14½ ounce) can chickpeas (drained, rinsed)
- ¼ cup tahini
- ¼ cup freshly squeezed lemon juice
- 3 tbsp extra-virgin olive oil
- 1 small garlic clove (peeled, halved)
- 1½ tsp fine sea salt
- 2 tsp smoked paprika
- 1 tsp ground coriander
- 1 tsp ground cumin

## Topping:

- ¼ cup toasted blanched almonds (roughly chopped)
- 2 tbsp flat-leaf parsley (roughly chopped)
- 2 tbsp virgin olive oil

**Directions:**

1. Using a metal fork, prick the skin of the sweet potato.

2. On high, microwave the potato for between 6-8 minutes, until fork tender.

3. Allow to cool for 15 minutes.

4. Peel and chop into cubes.

5. To make the hummus: Add the cooked and chopped sweet potato along with the chickpeas, tahini, lemon juice, olive oil, garlic, seas salt, smoked paprika, coriander and cumin to a food processor. Cover and process until silky smooth. Add a drop of water, if needed, to achieve our preferred consistency.

6. Cover and chill in the fridge for 2-4 hours.

7. When you are ready to serve, transfer the hummus to a serving plate.

8. Scatter the nuts over the top along with the parsley.

9. Drizzle with olive oil and serve with pita or veggie batons.

# Teriyaki Potatoes

A tasty Japanese-style side dish to enjoy with meat or poultry.

**Servings:** 6

**Total Time:** 25mins

**Ingredients:**

- 1½ pounds small red potatoes (cut into quarters)
- 1 tbsp butter
- 1 tbsp teriyaki sauce
- ¼ tsp garlic salt
- ¼ tsp Italian seasoning
- Dash of pepper
- Dash of cayenne pepper

**Directions:**

1. Add the potatoes to an ungreased microwave dish and dab with a little butter.

2. Add the teriyaki sauce, garlic salt, Italian seasoning, pepper, and cayenne pepper, tossing to coat.

3. Cover the dish and on high, microwave for 12-15 minutes, until the potatoes are bite tender. You will need to stir the mixture once or twice during cooking.

4. Serve.

# Desserts

# Banana Pudding

Satisfy those sweet cravings in a flash. This banana pudding
is the perfect dessert for anyone who needs to create a dessert
in a hurry.

**Servings:** 4-6

**Total Time:** 10mins

**Ingredients:**

- 3½ ounces butter (softened)
- 2 ripe bananas (peeled, divided)
- 3½ ounces light muscovado sugar
- 2 tsp ground cinnamon
- 3½ ounces self-raising flour
- 2 tbsp milk
- 2 eggs
- Icing sugar

**Directions:**

1. Add the butter to a microwave-safe casserole dish and on high, microwave for 30-60 seconds, until melted.

2. Add 1½ bananas and mash into the butter.

3. Next, add the sugar along with the cinnamon, flour, milk, and eggs and mix to combine.

4. Slice the remaining ½ banana over the top and return to the microwave oven. On high, cook until risen and cooked through, this will take approximately 8 minutes.

5. Dust the pudding with icing sugar and enjoy warm.

# Blackberry Cobbler

Berrylicious cobbler served with a helping of vanilla ice cream in just three minutes!

**Servings:** 1

**Total Time:** 3mins

**Ingredients:**

- ½ cup fresh blackberries
- 3 tbsp granulated sugar
- 1 tbsp butter
- ¼ cup unbleached all-purpose flour
- Pinch of salt
- ½ tsp baking powder
- 3 tbsp whole milk
- Vanilla ice cream (to serve)
- Honey (to drizzle)

**Directions:**

1. Add the blackberries to a large mug.

2. Sprinkle 1 tbsp sugar over the top and set to one side.

3. In the meantime, add the butter to a small microwave-safe bowl and microwave until melted; this will take between 15-20 minutes.

4. To the melted butter add the flour along with the remaining 2 tbsp sugar, salt, baking powder, and milk. Whisk until entirely incorporated.

5. Pour the batter over the berries in the mug and microwave, until the cobbler is cooked through and puffed up, approximately 2-3 minutes.

6. Serve with a dollop of ice cream and drizzle with honey.

# Caramel Custard

This creamy golden caramel custard makes a divine dinner-party dessert. Enjoy either warm or cold.

**Servings:** 6

**Total Time:** 25mins

**Ingredients:**

- ¾ cup sugar (divided)
- 2 tbsp water
- 4 eggs
- 2 tsp cornflour
- 1 tsp vanilla essence
- 2 cups whole milk

**Directions:**

1. Add ¼ cup of sugar along with the water to a dish, and uncovered cook on high for 2 minutes.

2. Remove from the microwave, stir and return to the microwave, uncovered for an additional 3-4 minutes until the sugar and water is a dark brown color. Set to one side.

3. In a bowl, beat the eggs with the cornflour, vanilla essence, and remaining sugar.

4. In a fine stream pour in the milk, continually beating.

5. Transfer the mixture to a dish and cover, cook at 30 percent for between 10-12 minutes, turning the pan halfway through.

6. Allow to cool before unmoulding.

7. Serve and enjoy.

# Chocolate Caramel Mug Cake

Dessert for one? In just six minutes you can chill-out and spoil yourself with this chocolaty mug cake.

**Servings:** 1

**Total Time:** 6mins

## Ingredients:

- 2 tbsp butter (melted)
- 4 tbsp granulated sugar
- ¼ tsp ground cinnamon
- 3 tbsp unsweetened cocoa powder
- 1 medium egg (beaten)
- ¼ tsp baking powder
- 4 tbsp all-purpose flour
- 3 tbsp whole milk
- 6 caramel squares (chopped)
- 3 tbsp semi-sweet chocolate chips
- Confectioner's sugar (to dust)

**Directions:**

1. Add the butter to a microwave-safe bowl and melt for 20 seconds.

2. In a 12-ounce mug, combine the sugar with the cinnamon, cocoa powder, egg, baking powder, flour, and milk and mix with a fork until incorporated.

3. Add the pieces of caramel followed by the chocolate chips.

4. In a 1000 watt microwave, cook for 70 seconds.

5. Remove from the microwave and allow the top to set.

6. Enjoy.

# Hazelnut Cake

Celebrate National Microwave Oven Day on December 6th with a portion of hazelnut cake.

**Servings:** 4

**Total Time:** 12mins

**Ingredients:**

- 1 cup refined flour
- ½ cup powdered sugar
- 1 tbsp baking powder
- 1 medium egg
- ½ cup refined oil
- ½ cup hazelnut spread
- 1 egg (whisked)

**Directions:**

1. In a microwave-safe bowl, sift in the refined flour, powdered sugar, and baking powder.

2. Crack the egg into a second bowl and whisk. Add the oil and hazelnut spread to the egg and whisk until the spread is combined.

3. Add the egg mixture to the dry ingredients and mix thoroughly. If the mixture is too thick add 2-3 tbsp of cold milk.

4. Transfer the bowl the microwave and cook in 30-second increments for approximately 2-3 minutes.

5. Serve.

# Lemon Pudding

A luscious citrus pudding is a refreshing dessert for all the family to enjoy.

**Servings:** 4

**Total Time:** 10mins

**Ingredients:**

- 3½ ounces caster sugar
- 3½ ounces butter (softened)
- 3½ ounces self-raising flour
- 2 medium eggs
- Zest of 1 lemon
- 1 tsp vanilla essence
- 4 tbsp lemon curd
- Crème fraiche (to serve)

**Directions:**

1. In a microwave-safe bowl, combine the sugar together with the butter, flour, eggs, lemon zest, and vanilla essence, stirring until creamy.

2. On high, microwave for 3 minutes until the pudding has risen and is set throughout, turning halfway through cooking. Allow to stand for 60 seconds.

3. In the meantime, in the microwave head the lemon curd for 30 seconds, stirring until smooth.

4. Pour the lemon curd over the top of the pudding and serve with crème fraiche.

# Lime Cheesecake

Enjoy this seriously good, zesty lime cheesecake in just 15 minutes, what more could you ask for?

**Servings:** 2-4

**Total Time:** 15mins

## Ingredients:

- ½ cup graham cracker crumbs
- 3 tbsp butter (melted)
- 1 tbsp sugar
- 8 ounces cream cheese (softened)
- ⅓ cup sugar
- Zest of 1 lime
- 2 tbsp freshly squeezed lime juice
- 1 medium egg
- Whipped cream (to serve)

**Directions:**

1. In a microwave-safe bowl, combine the cracker crumbs with the melted butter followed by 1 tbsp of sugar.

2. Divide the mixture evenly between 2-4 (1 cup) ramekins, firmly pressing the mixture into the bottom of the ramekins.

3. In a bowl, combine the cream cheese with the remaining sugar, lime zest, lime juice, and egg, mix until silky smooth and evenly divide the mixture between the jars until packed full.

4. Place the jars in the microwave for 2 minutes.

5. The surface of the cheesecake should look dry when sufficiently cooked. If it doesn't, microwave at 30-second increments until the tops are dry. This will take approximately 2½ minutes.

6. Transfer to the fridge to chill for 60 minutes and garnish with whipped cream.

7. Serve and enjoy.

# Mint Chocolate Bars

These minty bars are the perfect snack to pop in your lunchbox or to enjoy, at home, in school or on the move.

**Servings:** 6-8

**Total Time:** 30mins

**Ingredients:**

**Base:**

- Nonstick cooking spray
- ½ cup butter
- 1 cup sugar-free chocolate chips
- 1 cup almond flour

**Topping:**

- ¼ cup butter (softened)
- 6 tbsp heavy whipping cream
- 1 tsp peppermint essence
- 1 drop green food coloring
- ⅓ cup powdered sweetener

**Directions:**

1. Lightly grease an 8x6" square pan with cooking spray.

2. Add the butter and chocolate to a large microwave-safe bowl and on high, heat in the microwave for between 15-20 minutes. Stir until the butter and chocolate are entirely melted.

3. Add the flour and mix thoroughly.

4. Pat the mixture into the greased pan and transfer to the fridge.

5. In a small bowl, and using an electric mixer on moderate speed, beat the butter with the whipping cream, peppermint essence, and food coloring until well combined.

6. On a low-speed setting, gradually beat in the powdered sweetener until silky smooth.

7. Evenly spread the peppermint mixture over the chocolate mixture and transfer to the fridge to chill for 15-20 minutes.

8. When chilled slice into 5 rows by 5 rows to yield 25 bars.

# Old-Fashioned Rice Pudding

All the creamy taste and texture of good old-fashioned rice pudding but with none of the hassle.

**Servings:** 6

**Total Time:** 15mins

**Ingredients:**

- 3 eggs (beaten)
- 2 cups whole milk
- ⅓ cup sugar
- ¼ tsp salt
- 2 cups cooked pudding rice
- ½ cup raisins
- 1 tsp vanilla essence
- ¼ tsp cinnamon

**Directions:**

1. In a microwave-safe casserole dish combine the beaten eggs with the milk, sugar, and salt.

2. Stir in the cooked rice along with the raisins and vanilla essence.

3. Uncovered, on high, cook for between 8-10 minutes, stirring every 1-2 minutes.

4. Garnish with cinnamon and set aside to stand for half an hour, without stirring.

5. Serve warm.

# Pear Crisp

Indulge yourself with this fruity crisp and enjoy with custard or ice cream for a comforting warm dessert.

**Servings:** 1

**Total Time:** 4mins

**Ingredients:**

- 1 medium pear (peeled, cored, sliced)
- 2 tbsp brown sugar
- 2 tbsp quick-cooking oats
- 1 tbsp all-purpose flour
- ⅛ tsp ground cinnamon
- 1 tbsp butter (cold)
- Custard (to serve, optional)

**Directions:**

1. Add the pear to a microwave-safe bowl.

2. In a second bowl, combine the brown sugar with the oats, flour, and cinnamon.

3. Cut the butter in, until a crumbly consistency.

4. Sprinkle the mixture over the fruit, and uncovered, on high, microwave for 60-90 seconds until the fruit is tender.

5. Serve with warm custard.

# Author's Afterthoughts

*Thanks ever so much to each of my cherished readers for investing the time to read this book!*

*I know you could have picked from many other books but you chose this one. So a big thanks for downloading this book and reading all the way to the end.*

*If you enjoyed this book or received value from it, I'd like to ask you for a favor. Please take a few minutes to post an honest and heartfelt review on Amazon.com. Your support does make a difference and helps to benefit other people.*

*Thanks!*

**Daniel Humphreys**

# About the Author

*Daniel Humphreys*

Many people will ask me if I am German or Norman, and my answer is that I am 100% unique! Joking aside, I owe my cooking influence mainly to my mother who was British! I can certainly make a mean Sheppard's pie, but when it comes to preparing Bratwurst sausages and drinking beer with friends, I am also all in!

I am taking you on this culinary journey with me and hope you can appreciate my diversified background. In my 15 years career as a chef, I never had a dish returned to me by one of clients, so that should say something about me! Actually, I will take that back. My worst critic is my four years old son, who refuses to taste anything that is green color. That shall pass, I am sure.

My hope is to help my children discover the joy of cooking and sharing their creations with their loved ones, like I did all my life. When you develop a passion for cooking and my suspicious is that you have one as well, it usually sticks for life. The best advice I can give anyone as a professional chef is invest. Invest your time, your heart in each meal you are creating. Invest also a little money in good cooking hardware and quality ingredients. But most of all enjoy every meal you prepare with YOUR friends and family!

Printed in Great Britain
by Amazon

85816122R00079